# Spanish AMERICANS

## SPIRIT
of America®

# *Spanish* AMERICANS

## By Vicky Franchino

*Content Adviser: Susan DiGiacomo, Ph.D., Department of Anthropology, University of Massachusetts, Amherst, Massachusetts*

The Child's World®

*The Child's World®*
*Chanhassen, Minnesota*

7

# *Spanish*AMERICANS

*Published in the United States of America by The Child's World*®
P.O. Box 326 • Chanhassen, MN 55317-0326 • 800-599-READ • www.childsworld.com

*Acknowledgments*
   The Child's World®: Mary Berendes, Publishing Director

   Editorial Directions, Inc.: E. Russell Primm, Editorial Director; Pam Rosenberg, Line Editor; Katie Marsico,
   Assistant Editor; Matthew Messbarger, Editorial Assistant; Susan Hindman, Copy Editor; Susan Ashley,
   Proofreader; Julie Zaveloff, Chris Simms, and Peter Garnham, Fact Checkers; Tim Griffin/IndexServ, Indexer;
   Dawn Friedman, Photo Researcher; Linda S. Koutris, Photo Selector

   The Design Lab: Kathleen Petelinsek, Art Direction; Kari Thornborough, Page Production

*Photos*
   Cover/frontispiece: Spanish American residents of Mora, New Mexico, 1939.

   Cover photographs ©: Corbis; Gunter Marx Photography/Corbis.

   Interior photographs ©: Bettmann/Corbis: 7, 14, 15; Corbis: 6, 11 (Buddy Mays), 12 (Archivo Iconografico,
   S.A.), 13 (Christie's Images), 16, 17, 18, 19 (George H. H. Huey), 24 (Nik Wheeler), 25 (Reuters
   NewMedia Inc.); Getty Images: 26 (Allsport/Scott Halleran), 28 (Carlos Alvarez); Getty Images/Hulton
   Archive: 10, 20; Magnum Photos/Robert Capa R: 23; North Wind Picture Archives: 8.

*Library of Congress Cataloging-in-Publication Data*
   Franchino, Vicky.
     Spanish Americans / by Vicky Franchino.
        p. cm.—(Our cultural heritage)
     Includes index.
     Summary : Presents an overview of the heritage and culture of Spanish Americans and discusses their
   impact on American society.
     ISBN 1-59296-183-5 (lib. bdg. : alk. paper)
     1. Spanish Americans—Juvenile literature. [1. Spanish Americans.] I. Title. II. Series. E184.S75 F715 2004
   973'.0468—dc22                    2003018097

13              20              28

# *Contents*

# Chapter ONE

# *Exploring a New World*

MANY PEOPLE THINK THE BRITISH STARTED THE first colonies in the United States. The truth is that Spain came to America first. The Spanish explored many parts of North America and set up its oldest city—Saint Augustine, Florida—in 1565. This was many years before the English founded Jamestown (1607) or Plymouth (1620).

*The Spanish settlement of Saint Augustine during the 1600s; explorer Don Pedro Menéndez de Avilés is said to have sighted the coast of Florida on August 28, 1565, the feast day of Saint Augustine. Almost two weeks later, he and his troops came ashore, took over a small Indian village and named it Saint Augustine.*

The Spanish first came to the Americas in 1492. That year, a Genoese sailor named Christopher Columbus landed in what he believed was a new world. He had sailed west across the Atlantic Ocean in search of a shortcut to China, India, and the islands that today are known as the Republic of Indonesia. These places were the source of valuable spices that were scarce and extremely expensive in Europe. Traveling there east from Spain involved going over land, which was a difficult and often dangerous journey. Columbus hoped to sail west over what he thought was open water, reach the spice-rich countries of the East, and establish a new trade route. If successful, he would become a rich and famous man.

King Ferdinand and Queen Isabella of Spain sponsored Columbus's voyage. He readied three

*Of Columbus's three ships, the* Santa María *was the largest, followed in size by the* Pinta *(which was the fastest) and the* Niña.

7

ships—the *Santa Clara* (known as the *Niña* because it was owned by Juan Niño), the *Pinta,* and the *Santa María*—and set sail on August 3, 1492. Two months later, on October 12, Columbus and his men landed on the Caribbean island he called Hispaniola. Today, the countries of Haiti and the Dominican Republic occupy this island.

Columbus's surprising discovery caused great excitement in Spain. The country's rulers wanted to build an empire and claim land around the world. Many people hoped to find silver or gold in the new land. Others wanted to spread their religion to the native people. Spain sent **conquistadores** and **friars** to explore and settle the new land.

In the 1500s, the Spanish traveled to Mexico and declared it to be part of their empire. The Spanish also claimed a **peninsula** in the corner of the country. They called it *Baja California,* which means "lower California." Today, this peninsula

*Spanish friar Juan de Padilla discovering a cross left by explorer Francisco Vásquez de Coronado. The priest accompanied Coronado as he claimed large areas of present-day North America for Spain. Padilla was killed while attempting to preach Christianity to Native Americans.*

is part of Mexico. The area north of the peninsula was named *Alta California,* which means "upper California." Today, this area is the state of California. The name *California* probably came from a book written by a Spanish author of that time. In this book, California was a place "very close to paradise on earth."

The Spanish also explored the east and central areas of the new continent. In 1513, an explorer named Juan Ponce de León discovered Florida. It is said that he was looking for the "fountain of youth." This was supposed to be a magical spring of water that would keep people young forever. Instead, he found Florida. Because Ponce de León landed on Easter Sunday—known as *pascua florida* in Spanish—he named it Florida.

In the 1530s, the conquistadores traveled to the areas that are now Florida, Georgia, North and South Carolina, Tennessee, Alabama, Mississippi, Arkansas, and Louisiana. Between 1539 and 1542, an explorer named Francisco Vásquez de Coronado claimed a large area for Spain that is now the states of Texas, Oklahoma, Kansas, New Mexico, and Arizona. Coronado and his followers were the first Europeans to see the Grand Canyon.

Coronado was also one of the many explorers who searched for the Seven Cities of Cibola. These **legendary** cities were said to have streets

The early Spanish money used in North America was the real. If a person wanted to buy something but didn't have the right change, they would cut their reales into pieces! This is where we get the phrases "two bits," "four bits," and "pieces of eight."

9

*Coronado (on horseback) searches for the Seven Cities of Cibola. The explorer led about 300 Spanish soldiers, 1,000 American Indians, and several herds of sheep, pigs, and cattle on the famous journey through northern Mexico and the southwestern United States.*

paved with gold. Coronado never found the treasure he was looking for. Gold was found many years later in the Ortiz Mountains in New Mexico—an area Coronado traveled through!

During their first century in America, the Spanish spent most of their time exploring and hunting for riches. By 1700, the Spanish had sent more than 100 **expeditions** to North America.

SPAIN'S BASQUE COUNTRY IS IN THE WESTERNMOST PART OF THE PYRENEES Mountains and borders on the Bay of Biscay. Although it is part of Spain, the people of this area are very independent. Their culture is very old, and throughout history they have tried to keep their identity separate from Spain.

The people who live in the Basque Country call themselves Euskaldunak, which means "speakers of Euskara." Their language, Euskara, is unique. It does not have anything in common with Spanish or French, the two languages spoken in neighboring countries. Many Basques lived an isolated life, separated from other people. Traditionally, they were shepherds, farmers, sailors.

The first Basques in America came as sailors and soldiers. Many of the early Spanish expeditions included Basque men. In the early 1800s, educated Basques held many important positions in California.

More Basques began to immigrate to the United States in the mid-1800s. Most of these immigrants came from rural areas and did not have an education. Like other immigrants, they were looking for a better life. Often, they came to the United States in the hope of getting land.

Many of these early Basque immigrants were shepherds. They were drawn to the areas that are now Nevada, California, and Idaho. The mountains of these regions were similar to their homeland. Today, there are so many Basque people in Boise, Idaho, that it is sometimes called the Basque capital of America.

# Chapter Two

# Creating Spanish Settlements

THE SPANISH KNEW THEY WOULD NOT BE ABLE TO hold on to their land in North America unless Spanish citizens lived in their territories. So during the 1700s, Spain started to build more settlements. Some settlements were created by groups of Spaniards, native Mexicans, and mestizos, a mixed race created when a Spaniard and a Native American

*This South American painting shows a mestizo child with his Native American mother and Spanish father. Today, mestizos make up a large part of the population in countries such as Mexico, El Salvador, Honduras, Nicaragua, Colombia, Venezuela, and Chile.*

had children together. Many settlements were in what are now Texas, New Mexico, and California.

These colonies were usually very isolated. It could take months to travel from a settlement to the nearest city. People needed to rely on their families and their neighbors to survive. One thing that held them together was their great faith in God. Most of the colonists were followers of the Roman Catholic religion. Religious holidays and **ceremonies** were very important to them. Their priests were powerful leaders in the community.

The Spanish colonists were usually farmers. They grew wheat, barley, and corn. They also raised animals. Cattle and sheep were good animals to raise in the dry lands of the Southwest. The cattle were cared for by vaqueros, or cowboys. The vaqueros protected the cattle from thieves. They moved the herd to different areas so that they had enough grass to eat.

Other settlements started as missions. These were communities run by Roman Catholic priests. Some missions also had a presidio, a military fort, nearby. Soldiers at the presidio could protect the mission if it was attacked.

*A portrait of a vaquero painted by famous 19th-century artist Frederic Remington. These early cowboys rode horses and were so skilled at using a looped rope to catch cattle that some were believed to have roped animals from up to 60 feet (18 meters) away.*

13

Missions were popular with the Spanish government. The missions supported themselves. The money needed to set them up usually came from the Catholic Church. The missions grew their own food and often made or grew things like soap, olives, candles, and grapes, which could be sold for profit. The government also liked missions because they made it easier to control the Native Americans who lived in their territories.

The most famous Spanish missions were in California. Although Spain had control of California in the early 1500s, it didn't try to build settlements there until the 1760s. Around that time, Russian and British traders began to come to California. Spain was worried that another country would claim the area if Spain didn't settle it.

*Spanish missions in California and other southwestern states were not always happy places for Native Americans. In addition to sometimes being abused and held against their will, Indians from several different tribes were often housed together. This caused many individual traditions and customs to become mixed and lost over the years.*

Between 1769 and 1823, the Spanish built 21 missions on the coast of California. They covered a distance of about 600 miles (965 kilometers), from San Diego to Sonoma. Each mission was about one day's journey by horseback from the next. The road between them was called *El Camino Real,* or "the Royal Highway." Today, U.S. Highway 101 follows almost the same path as this original route.

*When Father Junípero Serra died at age 70 in 1784, he had traveled over 24,000 miles (38,624 kilometers) in his efforts to establish Catholic missions in the Americas.*

The missions were led by a man named Father Junípero Serra. Father Serra was a priest who had lived in New Spain—today's Mexico—since 1750. He had a very strong faith in God and wanted to share his Christian beliefs with the native people.

To start the missions, Father Serra made a very difficult journey from Mexico to California. He traveled over land. Another group of people traveled to the missions by ship. Each group suffered terrible hardships. Many became ill, and some died.

The priests brought the Native American people into the missions to work and live. Some came willingly, but others were forced to live at the mission. The priests believed they were saving the native people by teaching them about the Christian God. Many of them, however, were not happy living in the missions.

Life in the missions was very strict and different from the life the Native Americans were used to. Many families were split up, and everyone was expected to work very hard. Sometimes the Native Americans died from the new diseases that the Spanish had brought with them. Some of the people tried to run away. If they were found, they were cruelly punished.

*Art showing Native Americans making baskets and weaving rope on a California mission. While Indians frequently learned valuable skills from the mission priests, they were often worked so hard that observers compared them to slaves.*

The priests did teach them some valuable skills. The Native Americans learned how to make candles and tan animal hides. They learned how to grow new crops. Some learned how to speak Spanish. And some did become Christians willingly.

If a mission was successful, other people came to live near it. Over time, communities grew around these missions. These communities were known as pueblos. The cities of San Jose, Los Angeles, and Santa Cruz were once pueblos.

Spain planned for each mission to last about 10 years. During this time, the priests would teach the Native Americans how to run the community. The native people would become loyal Spanish citizens and then take over the mission. This plan was never followed. The Native Americans were never given control of the missions. The missions ended in a way that the Spanish had not expected.

*The Mission Dolores was founded in San Francisco, California, in 1776. It was the sixth mission to be established under Father Junípero Serra.*

THERE ARE MANY STATES WITH TIES TO SPAIN. SOME ARE WELL KNOWN; OTHERS might be surprising!

**California:** The missions are California's most well-known link to Spain. Today, many of them have been restored and are open to visitors.

**Arizona:** The Spanish built many missions in Arizona. The San Xavier del Bac Mission near Tucson is one of the most beautiful mission churches still standing. During the 1600s and 1700s, the Spanish mined silver and copper in Arizona.

**New Mexico:** Spanish names for cities, streets, and natural landmarks in New Mexico are more common than English names. Santa Fe, New Mexico's capital, was founded by the Spanish.

**Texas:** The Spanish first explored Texas in the 1500s and established missions there in the 1700s.

**Florida:** St. Augustine, Florida, founded in 1565, is the oldest city in the United States. Florida was a Spanish possession for 300 years.

**Massachusetts:** There are records showing that

Spanish explorers first came to this area in 1525—nearly 100 years before the Pilgrims arrived.

**South Carolina:** In 1526, Lucas Vásquez de Ayllón landed in South Carolina with 500 settlers. This colony, the first European settlement in North America, was abandoned within a few months.

**Alabama:** Mobile, Alabama was under Spanish rule for 33 years (1780–1813). Today, there are many street names and buildings that show the city's link to Spain.

**Louisiana:** Spanish explorers were the first Europeans to explore Louisiana. The city of New Orleans is home to many structures that were built by the Spanish.

# Chapter THREE

# Coming to the United States

*U.S. troops occupied Mexico City in 1847. Even though this meant that Mexico's capital city had been captured, it was several months before the war officially ended and Mexico surrendered territory to the United States.*

SPAIN'S POSITION IN THE NEW WORLD OF THE Americas changed in the 1800s. Mexico knew that the United States had won its independence from England. Many Mexicans wanted their country to be free, too. In 1810, Mexicans began to rebel against the Spanish leaders of their country. In 1821, they finally won their independence. All

of Spain's territories in North America became part of Mexico.

Mexico was not able to control all of the Spanish lands for long. Many U.S. citizens believed in **manifest destiny.** They thought they had a right to control all the land from the Atlantic Ocean to the Pacific Ocean. Much of the former Spanish territory now owned by Mexico was in this area. Between 1846 and 1848, Mexico and the United States fought a war. Mexico lost, and the Spanish territories became part of the United States. The people who lived in these areas had been Spanish citizens, then Mexican citizens. Now they became U.S. citizens.

During the rest of the 1800s, there was some immigration from Spain to the United States. Many of these immigrants were farmers. Like most immigrants, they hoped they would find a better life in America.

In 1898, the relationship between Spain and America worsened, and the two countries fought the Spanish-American War (1898). Very few people came from Spain to the United States during this time. After the United States won the war, it took Spain's territories in Cuba, Puerto Rico, Guam, and the Philippines. The Spanish empire had ended.

During the early 1900s, millions of Spanish immigrants came to the Americas, but most went

▸ The entire Spanish-American War was fought in less than one year. Spain declared war on the United States on April 24, 1898. The United States declared war on Spain the following day. The treaty that officially ended the war was signed on December 10, 1898, less than eight months after war was declared.

▶ Thousands of immigrants from the Spanish province of Asturias emigrated to the United States between 1900 and 1924. Asturias had been a mining center for thousands of years and many Asturian immigrants settled in West Virginia and other areas where they found work in the coal and zinc industries.

to South and Central America. Fewer than 100,000 Spanish immigrants came directly to the United States. Some thought they would find a better life in the United States and stayed in the country. Others only planned to stay until they had enough money to return and make a better life in Spain.

The trip from Spain to the United States was expensive and very difficult. Some families had to borrow money for the trip. They had to work hard to pay the money back. The ships that the immigrants traveled on were dirty and crowded. Sickness spread quickly, and some passengers died during the voyage.

Many of the Spanish immigrants settled in New York, California, and Florida. There were already Spanish communities in these areas, so it was easy for the new immigrants to feel at home. Others went to **industrial** areas in Illinois, Michigan, Ohio, or Pennsylvania, or they worked in the coal mines in West Virginia. Many people from the Basque Country settled in the mountainous areas of Idaho and California.

Spaniards from Andalusia—the most southern region of Spain—were hired to work on Hawaiian sugar plantations. They came to Hawaii between 1907 and 1913. Most of them eventually moved to California.

Although there were never many immigrants from Spain, after 1921 there were even fewer. The U.S. government set up a quota system. This meant

that only a certain number of immigrants would be allowed to come to the United States from any country. Between 1930 and 1940, the number of Spanish immigrants in the United States decreased. Many of the Spanish people living in America returned to Spain or moved to other countries.

As a result of the Spanish **Civil War** (1936–1939), many political **refugees** fled Spain. Most went to other European countries, and many found freedom in Mexico and other Latin American countries. After this war, few Spaniards were allowed to immigrate to the United States. During the 1940s and 1950s, Spain had many problems and the people were very poor. In the 1960s, more people from Spain were allowed to come to the United States. Almost 50,000 people came to escape the poverty in their country. As conditions in Spain improved, fewer people immigrated to the United States.

*Spanish refugees, such as the ones shown here, faced several difficult challenges after the Spanish Civil War. Unable to stay in their home-land, they were often forced to flee to other European countries. Thousands of Spaniards were imprisoned in refugee camps in southern France, where they suffered from hunger and disease.*

# Spanish Contributions to American Culture

AMERICA IS OFTEN CALLED A MELTING POT. THE United States is a land of immigrants, and its traditions are really a mix of the traditions of people from many countries.

There are many examples of Spanish culture in the United States today. But it can be difficult to tell if something is truly Spanish or if it comes from a Latin American country such as Mexico or Cuba. Even though these countries are separate today, at one time they were all linked. Spain was once one of the most powerful countries in the world and claimed much of the land in today's North, Central, and South America.

It is because of Spain, that Spanish is the second most common language in many cities across the United States. Many of the people who speak Spanish are actually from Mexico, but Spain had controlled their country for about 300 years.

Many cities in the United States have Spanish names because they were founded by the Spanish. Some of the most famous are San Antonio, Texas; Santa Fe, New Mexico; Tucson, Arizona; and Los Angeles, California.

Many common English words have Spanish roots. Some examples are: alligator, cigar, rodeo, tornado, hurricane, patio, tobacco, guerrilla, plaza, ranch, lasso, corral, and mesa.

Although foods such as tacos and burritos are very common in the United States, they are not truly from Spain. Paella is a delicious dish that is Spanish. It is made of rice, vegetables, and meat or fish. Another Spanish dish, gazpacho, makes a wonderful meal on a hot day. Gazpacho is a cold soup made with tomatoes, vegetables, and olive oil.

Jai alai is a sport that originated in the Basque Country of northern Spain and is popular in some areas with large Hispanic populations. This game is played on a court and is similar to squash or handball.

*Two athletes enjoy a game of jai alai in Tampa Bay, Florida. In the Basque language, jai alai means "merry festival." This is because the various games from which jai alai developed were often played at festivals and celebrations in Spain more than 300 years ago.*

*FIESTA* IS THE SPANISH WORD FOR A PARTY OR CELEBRATION. SOME FIESTAS are part of Christian religious celebrations. Other fiestas are simply for fun. Today, the following religious fiestas occur in Spanish communities across the United States:

### Las Posadas

This celebration is in memory of the birth of Jesus. Christians believe that Jesus is the son of God. Before Jesus was born, his mother, Mary, and her

husband, Joseph, went from inn to inn looking for a place to stay. The people at this celebration go from door to door singing. They carry lanterns to light their way. They are looking for a place that has room for Mary and Joseph. Sometimes the people sing or carry small statues of Mary and Joseph. Las Posadas traditionally started on December 16 and went on for nine nights. Today, the fiesta is usually held on Christmas Eve, the night before Christmas. At the end of the journey, there is food and a piñata. A piñata is a decorated pot or papier-mâché container filled with candy. The children are blindfolded and take turns hitting the piñata until it breaks.

*The Day of the Three Kings*
January 6 is the traditional day that Christians celebrate the arrival of the Three Kings. These were the three men who traveled to bring gifts to the baby Jesus. On this holiday children leave their shoes outside. They put straw in their shoes in memory of Jesus sleeping in a **manger.** During the night, the three Kings come and leave fruit, candy, and small toys.

*Easter*
Christians around the world celebrate Easter. This is the day they celebrate their belief that Jesus rose from the dead. Easter is a celebration of new life. Some people celebrate with special cakes. Others make *cascarones* (kahs-kah-RO-nays). These are hollow eggs that are dyed and filled with confetti.

Enrique Iglesias is a popular Spanish-American singer and songwriter. He was born in Madrid, Spain, but has lived in Miami, Florida, since he was seven years old. He has won many awards for his music. Actor Antonio Banderas was born in Málaga, Spain. His first big role in the United States was in the film *Philadephia*. Scientist Luís Álvarez won the 1968 Nobel Prize in physics. Álvarez was one of the scientists who worked on the Manhattan Project to develop the first atomic bomb. He was also the first scientist to say that dinosaurs may have been killed because a meteorite hit the earth. Astronaut Miguel López Alegría was born in Madrid, Spain, but was raised in the United States. He is now a U.S. citizen and works for NASA.

These famous Spanish Americans and thousands of others are part of the large group of Americans with ancestors from Spain. The Spanish Americans who make the United States their home today continue to enrich the lives of all citizens of their adopted country.

*Popular musician Enrique Iglesias at the 2002 Onda Music Awards in Barcelona, Spain. Enrique's father, Julio Iglesias, is also a famous musician.*

**1492**   Christopher Columbus sails across the Atlantic Ocean from Spain and lands on an island that is now home to Haiti and the Dominican Republic.

**1513**   Juan Ponce de León lands in Florida and claims it for Spain.

**1539–1542**   Francisco Vásquez de Coronado explores the present-day states of Texas, Oklahoma, Kansas, New Mexico, and Arizona, claiming them for Spain.

**1565**   The city of St. Augustine, Florida, is founded.

**1769–1823**   Spanish missionaries build 21 missions on the coast of California.

**1821**   Mexico wins its independence from Spain.

**1846–1848**   The Mexican War is fought, and the United States takes control of much of the former Spanish territory from Mexico.

**1898**   The Spanish American War is fought, and the United States takes control of Spanish territories in Cuba, Puerto Rico, Guam, and the Philippines.

**1907**   Spaniards from the Andalusia region are hired to work on Hawaiian sugar plantations.

**1936–1939**   The Spanish Civil War is fought.

**1968**   Luís Álvarez wins the Nobel Prize for physics.

**ceremonies (SER-uh-moh-nees)**
Ceremonies are formal events with special actions, words, and music that are held to celebrate a special occasion. Religious ceremonies were very important to the early Spanish settlers.

**civil war (SIV-il WOR)**
A civil war is a war between different groups of people within a country. During the Spanish Civil War, very few Spaniards immigrated to the United States.

**conquistadores (kon-KEES-tah-dor-es)**
Conquistadores were men who were sent to the Americas by Spain to explore the land and conquer the native people. The conquistadores were the first Europeans to explore many regions of North America.

**expeditions (ek-spuh-DISH-uhns)**
Expeditions are long journeys for the purpose of exploring. Spain sponsored many expeditions to the New World.

**friars (FRY-ers)**
Friars are men who are members of a religious order. Spanish friars started missions throughout North America.

**industrial (in-DUHSS-tree-uhl)**
Something that is industrial is related to business and factories. Many Spanish immigrants found work in the industrial Midwest.

**legendary (LEJ-uhn-dary)**
Something that is legendary has some basis in fact but is not completely true. The Seven Cities of Cibola were legendary cities.

**manger (MAYN-jur)**
A manger is a box that holds food for animals to eat. Hispanic children put straw in their shoes on The Day of the Three Kings to remind them of Jesus' birth in a manger.

**manifest destiny (MAN-ih-fest DESS-tuh-nee)**
Manifest destiny is the belief that a future event must happen. During the 1800s, U.S. citizens believed it was their manifest destiny to control the land from the Atlantic Ocean to the Pacific Ocean.

**peninsula (puh-NIN-suh-luh)**
A peninsula is a piece of land that sticks out from another, larger landmass and is almost completely surrounded by water. Baja California is a peninsula of Mexico.

**refugees (REF-yuh-jees)**
Refugees are people who are forced to leave their home country to escape danger. At the end of the Spanish Civil War, many refugees went to other parts of Europe.

## Web Sites

Visit our homepage for lots of links about Spanish Americans:
**http://www.childsworld.com/links.html**

*Note to Parents, Teachers, and Librarians:*
We routinely verify our Web links to make sure they're safe,
active sites—so encourage your readers to check them out!

## Books

Anderson, Dale. *The California Missions.* Milwaukee, Wis.: World Almanac Library, 2002.

Berendes, Mary. *Spain.* Chanhassen, Minn.: The Child's World, 1999.

Rogers, Lura. *Spain.* New York: Children's Press, 2001.

Stein, R. Conrad. *In the Spanish West.* New York: Benchmark Books, 2000.

## Places to Visit or Contact

**Mission San Juan Capistrano**
*To visit a mission and learn more about the history of Spanish missions in California*
Ortega Highway and Camino Capistrano
San Juan Capistrano, CA 92693

**Statue of Liberty and Ellis Island Immigration Museum**
*To learn more about the history of immigration to the United States*
National Park Service
Statue of Liberty National Monument and Ellis Island
New York, NY 10004

# Index

## About the Author

VICKY FRANCHINO HAS ALWAYS LOVED TO LEARN ABOUT THE PAST. SHE HAS fond memories of Laura Ingalls Wilder's "Little House" books–especially *The Long Winter*–and still has a picture of the papier-mâché castle she made in the 6th grade. Vicky is excited to be part of the Spirit of America series. She thoroughly enjoyed the chance to learn more about the immigrants who have worked together to create the United States that we know today. Vicky lives with her husband and their three daughters in Wisconsin, and hopes that her children will enjoy learning about the past as much as she does!